For aLL the curious expLorers – M.M.

PUFFIN BOOKS

UK | USA | Canada | Ireland | Australia | India | New Zealand | South Africa

Puffin Books is part of the Penguin Random House group of companies whose addresses can be found at global.penguinrandomhouse.com.

www.penguin.co.uk   www.puffin.co.uk   www.ladybird.co.uk

Penguin
Random House
UK

First published 2021

001

Text copyright © Maddie Moate, 2021
Illustrations copyright © Paul Boston, 2021
Author photo copyright © Elodie Giuge

The moral right of the author and illustrator has been asserted

All opinions are the author's own or those of experts. The author has taken great care to check factual accuracy and secure permission to use expert content.

The information in this book is intended as a general guide and is believed to be correct as at July 2021. The recipes may not be suitable for those with certain food allergies or intolerances. Please check the ingredients in the recipes carefully if you have any allergies and, if in doubt, consult a health professional. Adult supervision is required at all times and always use appropriate kitchen safety measures. The activities are for informational or entertainment purposes only. The author and publishers disclaim, as far as the law allows, any liability arising directly or indirectly from the use or misuse of any information contained in this book.

Printed in China

The authorized representative in the EEA is Penguin Random House Ireland, Morrison Chambers, 32 Nassau Street, Dublin D02 YH68

A CIP catalogue record for this book is available from the British Library

ISBN: 978–0–241–48943–7

All correspondence to:
Puffin Books, Penguin Random House Children's
One Embassy Gardens, 8 Viaduct Gardens, London SW11 7BW

STUFF

Maddie Moate

Illustrated by Paul Boston

PUFFIN

Hi, I'm Maddie,

Thank you so much for picking up my book! If you love adventure, caring for the planet and finding out how things are made, then you're in for a treat.

I have always been fascinated by the way things are made and have spent the last 5 years visiting factories, farms and workshops to explore their inner workings and learn how people make the stuff we use every day. I've been lucky to share my discoveries online and on television, but now I get to do it in this book!

During my adventures, I've come to realize that everything we use and all the stuff we own has a story. A beginning, a middle and an end.

Where does it come from? How was it made? And what will happen to it?

The stories our things tell us have meaning because they impact the world around us. We don't always think about this story when we make, use and throw away our stuff. But when we do, when we *really* think about the way something is made and the effect it could have on our planet, the most ordinary thing can suddenly become . . . **extra**ordinary.

What if paper could be made with elephant poo?

What if trains could levitate?

What if ink could be made with pollution . . .

. . . and fences made with beehives?

Across the planet, now and throughout history, people and communities have invented everyday objects in the most creative, caring and often mind-blowing ways!

I find these global tales really inspiring, which is why I wanted to share some of my favourite stories across these precious pages. You're about to go on a worldwide eco-tour of STUFF!

Some of the places you'll read about I've been to, others I'm yet to visit, but in this book we can travel the world together! See if you can spot me as you flip through the pages.

So, let's get started! Over the page you'll find a map to help guide you on your journey.

Where do you want to go first?

Stay curious,

Maddie

Stuff to make and do

All these stories have made me think about what I can make and reuse at home. Check out some ideas on pages 46–49 and have a go – maybe you could invent something new, reused and fantastic yourself!

Stuff you might need to know

Throughout this book there are a few **extra-special words** and **phrases**, which you may or may not have heard of before. They are extra-special as understanding them helps us better support our planet. You can find these **words** and their descriptions on pages 50–52.

REDUCE
REUSE
RECYCLE

Stuff to spot!

When I'm on my travels, I love to explore, look around and see what I can spot! I enjoy spotting things in books, too, so see what you can discover in my 'Spotter's Guide to *Stuff*' on page 53.

EXTRAordinary Stuff Around the World

Thunder Bread
(Iceland)
page 12

T-shirt Trends
(UK)
page 28

3D Space Printing
(USA)
page 24

Super Salad
(UK)
page 34

North America

Seaweed Wraps
(USA)
page 30

Plant Power
(Polynesia)
page 14

Central America

Eco-bricks
(Guatemala)
page 26

Africa

South America

Meatless Burgers
(worldwide)
page 40

Fog Catchers
(Peru)
page 18

Worm Tea Compost
(worldwide)
page 36

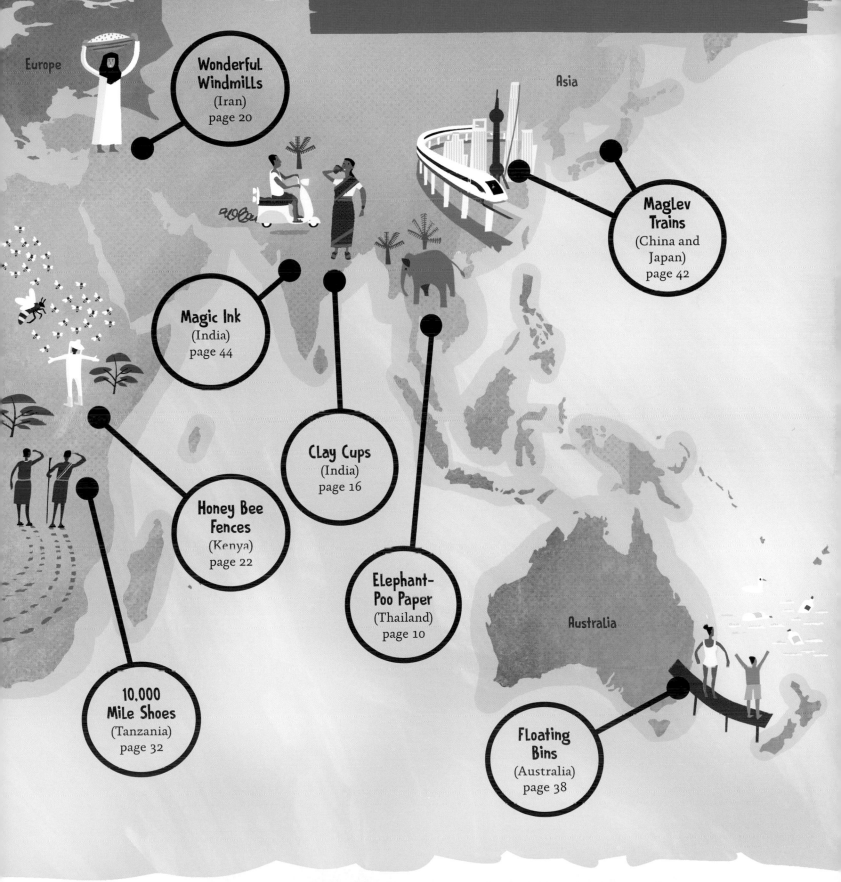

It doesn't matter if we live in a bustling city, in the sweeping countryside or in the foothills of mountains – we all need STUFF!

People have come up with some pretty amazing ways to get stuff made and to reduce our impact on the environment. The stories of these inventions are as inspiring as they are spectacular. Take a look at this map to discover them for yourself!

Europe

Asia

Wonderful Windmills
(Iran)
page 20

MagLev Trains
(China and Japan)
page 42

Magic Ink
(India)
page 44

Clay Cups
(India)
page 16

Honey Bee Fences
(Kenya)
page 22

Elephant-Poo Paper
(Thailand)
page 10

Australia

10,000 MiLe Shoes
(Tanzania)
page 32

FLoating Bins
(Australia)
page 38

Elephant-Poo Paper

Have you ever wondered where paper comes from? Today, most paper is made from wood and recycled paper products, but paper can also be made from rice, coconuts, old cotton clothes and even . . . elephant poo!

All these things start their lives as plants and are made up of something called **plant fibre**.

Plant fibres are hair-like threads that help give a plant its shape. If you tear apart a banana leaf or the husk of a coconut, you'll see these stringy fibres inside. If you mush the plant fibres with water and spread the mixture on to a sheet, the material dries and becomes a piece of paper!

  =

tree bark   coconuts   rice plants   banana leaves   plant fibres

How do you make paper from poo?

Elephants eat lots and lots and LOTS of plants. An Indian elephant might spend up to 19 hours a day eating and can chow down around 150 kg of food (that's about the same weight as an adult gorilla!) – the bulk of which is made up of plant fibres.

poo shed

elephant dung

However, fibre is tricky to digest and elephants have pretty bad digestive systems. In fact, they only digest a quarter to a half of all their food, so lots of it comes out looking the same as when it went in! All that food means a lot of poo and they can poop 15–20 times a day! That's an awful lot of fibre-packed dung that can be put to good use.

In Chiang Mai, northern Thailand, there is an elephant-poo paper factory tucked neatly away in the jungle. Here they work closely with an elephant sanctuary to make lots of poo paper!

You might imagine this would be really smelly, but elephants are **herbivores** and only eat plants so their dung doesn't smell bad at all.

First the poo has to be rinsed and cleaned to get rid of any nasty bugs and germs . . .

cleaning drums

fresh water and poo fibres

. . . then it is boiled in a bubbling cauldron for 6 hours . . .

. . . and left to dry out in the sun.

food dye (for colour)

mixing machine

The dried poo then goes in a mixing machine, which works just like a smoothie maker! Everything is chopped and whisked together into a sloppy wet paste we call **pulp**.

The wet pulp is squeezed into balls the size of apples. Each ball of pulp will make one large sheet of paper!

balls of pulp

mesh frame

The pulp is then spread on to a mesh frame and left to dry.

After it is dry, the brand-new piece of poo paper can be peeled off the frame.

tray

Find out how to make your own recycled paper on page 46.

The money made from selling the paper goes towards planting more food, like banana leaves, for the elephants – so the system works in a big loop, and there's barely any waste.

Save our trees!

Making paper from wood means cutting down lots of trees. **Deforestation** disturbs animals and can contribute towards **climate change**. **Sustainable** wood pulp can be great for making smooth, white paper, but most of the time we use paper for notes, scribbles or arts and crafts. So, if we don't need PERFECT paper all the time, then why don't we make more paper from a waste product like poo instead?!

Thunder Bread

Did you know it's possible to bake bread on the shores of an icy lake? Much of our food is prepared in factories and transported all over the world, which uses a lot of energy. However, this isn't always the case...

In the small Icelandic village of Laugarvatn, people have been baking bread in the most curious way for at least 100 years. The traditional *hverabrauð* is a special kind of rye bread that is baked in a hot spring!

Uppskrift Ömmu (Grandma's recipe)

Ingredients:
4 cups of rye flour
2 cups of plain flour
2 cups of sugar
A pinch of salt
4 teaspoons of baking powder
1.2 litres of milk

Method:
1. Line a metal pot with butter
2. Mix all the ingredients together in a mixing bowl
3. Pour the mixture into the metal pot and put on the lid
4. Seal the pot with kitchen foil
5. Bury in the sand 30cm below the surface and mark the spot with a stone
6. Bake in the hot spring for 24 hours
7. Dig up the pot and cool with cold water from the lake
8. Turn out the baked bread from the pot
9. Slice the bread and serve warm with slabs of butter and slices of smoked herring

Amma X

How do you bake bread in a hot spring?

A baker leaves the comfort of home, braving the cold to make her way to work. Carrying a spade and a cooking pot full of dough, the baker trudges across the icy shore, until she sees hot steam rising from the ground. She puts her ear close to the sand and listens to the gentle bubbling of a hot spring.

The baker digs a hole about 30cm deep and it quickly fills with boiling water...

hot spring

cooking pot

steam

sand

...then the pot of dough is put into the natural oven and covered with sand.

It is left to bake for 24 hours, and when it comes out of the hot spring, a fresh loaf of *hverabrauð* is ready!

What is a hot spring?

A hot spring is made when water that has trickled deep into the ground is heated by hot molten rock called **magma**. The water gets so hot that it bubbles back to the surface at temperatures as high as 100°C. Magma oozes beneath the Earth's crust, in one of the many layers that make up our planet – it's a bit like a cake!

The top layer that we live on is called the **crust**.

The crust is broken up into slow-moving rocky pieces called **tectonic plates**. They fit together like a planet-sized jigsaw puzzle! Where tectonic plates meet at a boundary, you often find hot springs and volcanoes.

The layer underneath the crust is called the **mantle**. The mantle contains magma, hot molten rock that can ooze like runny plastic.

Below the mantle is a liquid layer called the **outer core**.

When magma rises up from the mantle, it sometimes creates a **magma chamber** close to the Earth's surface. This is what heats the groundwater and makes a hot spring.

The centre of the planet is called the **inner core**. It is the hottest part of the Earth – over 5,000°C!

Iceland has lots of hot springs because it sits on top of a **tectonic plate boundary**. We call the heat we use from inside the Earth *geothermal energy*, and the best thing about it is that it's renewable!

The Icelanders nickname rye bread *þrumari* (thunder bread) because some say that eating too much can cause a serious case of *bottom* thunder! *Parp!*

Others will tell you the nickname comes from a Norse god, as rye bread is served at Thorrablot, a Viking festival that honours Thor, the god of thunder.

Hot topics

For hundreds of years Icelanders have used geothermal energy for cooking, bathing and heating their homes, but more recently humans have engineered ways to convert this heat into electrical energy. It's even being used to power greenhouses so that fruits, such as tomatoes, can be grown all year round! This *renewable energy* is a resource with lots of exciting potential for the future of our planet.

Plant Power

Did you know that plants have sailed the seas for hundreds of years? Around 1,700 years ago, the ancient Polynesians set sail on voyages of discovery in hand-made canoes.

They carried botanical toolkits – a collection of seeds or cuttings known as **canoe plants**. When the Polynesians arrived on a new island, they could grow everything they needed!

Plants are still incredibly important as a human resource. Not only do we eat them, but we also use them for medicine, construction, packaging and so much more!

Bamboo

Bamboo is strong and lightweight, and grows faster than any other plant on the planet. Some species can grow up to 1 metre in 24 hours! This makes it very useful for growing building materials quickly.

Gourd

This thick-skinned vegetable makes a great food and water container when it's dried and hollowed out. Gourds can also be decorated and filled with seeds or pebbles to make rattling instruments.

Turmeric

The bright orange underground stem of a turmeric plant is called a **rhizome** and is used as a cooking spice and a natural dye to colour fabrics.

Pinecone ginger

This ginger oozes a clear foamy slime that can be used as shampoo!

canoe

canoe plants

seeds

cuttings

Home sweet home

Have a look at this hut. Would you believe me if I told you that EVERY PART of it has been made from just one type of plant? The coconut tree! The coconut tree was a very important ancient Polynesian canoe plant. In fact, it's so good that people all over the planet still use it to make lots of stuff today!

See how many things you can discover on this page. Imagine if we all used **natural resources** to make more of our everyday stuff – there'd be a lot less plastic and **pollution** in the world.

roof

walLs

From the wood:

fire

From the Leaves:

baskets

building materials

mats

From the stems and branches:

broomsticks

From the coconut water:

'Nata de coco' – a sweet jelly

From the shell:

bowls

cups

From the coconut:

flour

oil

miLk

shampoo

Lip baLm

From the roots:

toothbrushes

mouthwash

dye

From inside the stem:

'Heart of palm' – a vegetable

From the sap:

sugar

Clay Cups

Did you know that people throw away their cups all over the world?
They slurp hot drinks out of plastic cups, only to chuck them in the bin moments later where they rarely get recycled. But if you were to drink a cup of *masala chai* by a roadside in Kolkata, India, you'd likely be served this sweet and spicy tea in a handcrafted clay cup called a *bhar*.

As you sip your warm, milky drink, you might be surprised to see a tea-drinking neighbour throw their empty cup on the ground and crush it into thousands of muddy pieces. This may seem wasteful, but it is much better for the environment than **single-use plastic**.

The clay cups of Kolkata

Tea drinking is a very important part of life in India. Many people will stop at a *chai wallah*, a local roadside tea seller, several times a day. With so much tea drinking going on, the country needs an awful lot of cups!

Kolkata is one of the few cities where clay cups are still used and sculpted by local potters.

মশলা চা

MASALA CHAI
Spiced Tea

milk

black tea

sugar
(or sweetener)

cinnamon

ginger

How is a bhar made?

Potteries in Kolkata are often family-run businesses. The clay comes from the Hooghly River.

It is scooped up from the riverbeds when the tide is out . . .

. . . then loaded on to boats or lorries to be carried into the city.

potter's wheel

At the pottery, the gritty river clay is squished and squeezed till it is smooth and mouldable.

A lump of clay is thrown on to a spinning potter's wheel and sculpted into a cup shape. The potter works VERY quickly, making as many as 4,000 cups a day.

drying cups

The wet cups are left to dry in the sun.

kiln

Once they are dry, the cups are baked in a kiln until they are hard and turn a reddish pink colour.

Making *bhar* is an ancient tradition, and a skill passed down through generations. Not all communities have skilled potters working hard to make throw away teacups, so what can we use instead? Rather than a single-use plastic cup, we could carry a reusable cup or bottle that we can use again and again! *Find out how on page 48.*

Every morning the dainty cups are delivered to the thousands of tea stalls that line Kolkata's streets, ready for a busy day ahead. Each will be filled with *masala chai* before being smashed on the ground, where it'll slowly wash back to the river from where it came.

Why are clay cups good for the planet?

Clay cups are environmentally friendly because they are made of a natural material that easily crumbles back into earth. However, single-use plastic cups are used around the world. In fact, the UK throws away around 2.5 BILLION plastic-coated cups every year. Unlike clay, plastic takes hundreds of years to break down – so we need to look for alternatives.

Fog Catchers

How do you find water in a desert? High in the mountains around Lima, Peru, the slopes are often covered in thick, gloomy mist. Despite the cold fog, Lima is a desert landscape where it hardly ever rains. This is a big problem when you need clean running water. So the Peruvians have found a way to capture precious droplets of water out of the sky.

This is known as **fog catching**.

net

fog

Water – a precious resource

When we are thirsty, most of us can go to the kitchen, turn on the tap and pour ourselves a glass of drinking water. But this simple luxury isn't always possible for people living in some of the poorest communities across the globe.

How can this be when most of the Earth is covered by water? Surely there's plenty to go around? Well, salty sea water is very different from the fresh water humans need for drinking, cooking, washing and growing things. So it can be really tricky when there's not enough.

There are 2 million people living on the outskirts of Lima whose homes are not connected to water pipes. The lack of rainfall and fresh water is a real issue, so they have to be inventive and find water where they can.

What is fog?

Fog is just like a cloud, but it hangs close to the ground instead of being high in the sky. When the sun heats the Earth's water, some of that water evaporates. It turns from a liquid into an invisible gas called **water vapour**. As the water vapour rises, it cools and turns back into tiny microdroplets of water. This is called **condensation**.

These microdroplets gather round bits of dust in the air, and we see them as clouds or fog. (Clouds might look fluffy, but if you were to walk through one, you'd actually get very wet!)

How does a fog catcher work?

A fog catcher is a large mesh net, hung between two posts on the side of a foggy mountain. (It looks a bit like a volleyball net for giants!)

When the wind blows, the fog is pushed into the mesh net, which traps the microdroplets of water in the air.

As more and more tiny droplets bump into each other, they get bigger and heavier.

The big droplets trickle all the way

to
the
bottom
of
the
net

where they drip into a channel made from a pipe.

This collects the water and sends it to a storage container.

When the weather conditions are just right, a single fog catcher in Lima can collect up to 400 litres of water a day. That's about the same amount of water we'd use for 5 baths!

pipe

storage container

The water is shared between local families, who use it in their allotments so they can grow fresh food. It can also be used for showering, washing the dishes and, if it is filtered, it can be used as drinking water.

Hopefully, one day, more homes will be connected to a water network so that fresh water can be enjoyed straight from a tap. But, until then, the fog catchers have given many people a smart and *sustainable* source of water.

Wonderful Windmills

sail

windmill

What do you think of when you imagine a windmill?

You might picture four wooden sails spinning on top of a pretty building. This would be a Dutch windmill: the kind that has become a well-known symbol of the Netherlands. However, some of the world's oldest windmills are actually found in Iran.

The city of Nashtifan in north-eastern Iran is known for being extremely windy. Strong winds blow throughout the year and, at times, can reach speeds of 100km per hour or more! Whoosh!

Protecting the townspeople from the whip-like winds is a long, towering wall that houses some incredible inventions – 24 vertical windmills, called *asbad*, that are used to grind grain into flour.

It's estimated that these windmills were built over 1,000 years ago. They are made from **natural resources** like clay, straw, wood and stone. Extraordinarily, even after all this time, some of them still work today!

Thanks to Nashtifan's ancient engineers, the wind that could have been a danger to the city has become its most useful and prized asset.

straw

stone

wood

How do the windmills work?

Each windmill is made up of six sails connected to a central pole (or shaft) inside a vertical chamber. This shaft is attached to two enormous stone discs called **millstones**.

When the wind blows through the chamber, the air pushes the sails round and round . . .

. . . and makes the shaft and top millstone turn, too. The heavy millstone grinds the grain and turns it into flour.

Why are the Nashtifan windmills so smart?

The windmills protect the city from gusting winds but, more importantly, they use wind power to make flour that can be baked into breads such as *sangak*, a delicious Iranian flatbread.

The best thing about wind power is that it's a type of **renewable energy**. The wind keeps on blowing and will always be part of our climate, so it will always be there to give us energy.

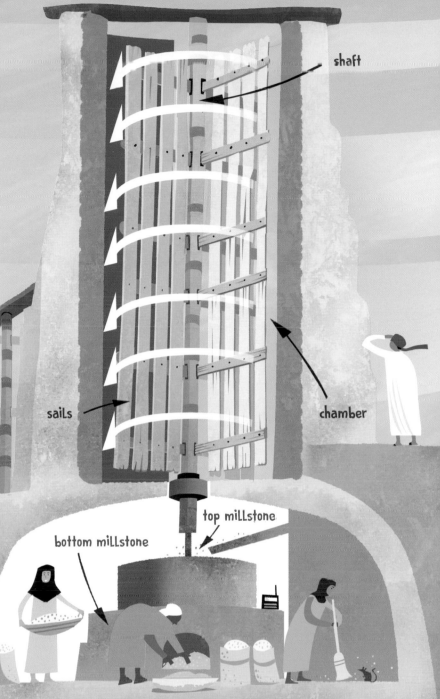

shaft

sails

chamber

top millstone

bottom millstone

The ancient people of Nashtifan used renewable energy, and we need to do the same.

At the moment we still use a lot of **non-renewable energy** like **fossil fuels**. To get energy from fossil fuels, we have to burn them. This produces **greenhouse gases** that go into the atmosphere and trap heat, causing **global warming**, which contributes to **climate change**. One option is to use wind turbines – a kind of modern windmill that produces electricity.

If we use more renewable energy from the wind, the waves and sunlight, we will have a better chance of stopping global warming and slowing down climate change.

← wind turbine

Honey Bee Fences

How can you keep out a hungry elephant?

In Kenya, African elephants are free to roam. A herd will travel great distances in search of food. But, in recent years, they have had less room to wander as humans have built more roads, railways, farms and buildings.

Elephants are **herbivores**, which means they eat plants (a LOT of plants), so if they come across a small farm, they will tuck into its delicious crops. It's an easy meal for them, but a big problem for the local people. Farmers used to try to scare the elephants away to protect their farmland. However, this made the animals cross and confused, which was dangerous for both the humans and the elephants.

A buzzing idea

Scientists and **conservationists** worked with local people in northern Kenya to find a peaceful solution to the elephant-sized problem. They found it in the buzzing of a tiny African honey bee!

For many years local tribespeople had believed that elephants were scared of honey bees. To test this idea, scientists played the sound of buzzing bees to a group of elephants, and watched and waited . . .

When the elephants heard the noise, they shook their ears to fend off the phantom bees and quickly moved away.

They also made low rumbling sounds to warn other herds, and this noise has since been called **the bee rumble**.

It was this experiment that led to the idea of beehive fences!

beehive

Fence posts are positioned around the farm . . .

. . . and simple beehives are hung up on a long wire.

If an elephant walks into the wire, all the hives start to swing. This disturbs the bees, who zoom out of the hives to protect their **queen bee** and chase away the elephant.

The bees might bother or sting the elephant, but they won't cause it any long-term harm. The elephant learns not to come too close to the farm and the farmers are able to safely protect their crops.

22

Beehive benefits

The beehive fences encourage local farmers to take on the role of beekeepers so they can harvest the honey. This honey can be used in their own cooking or sold at the market. Any excess beeswax left over from harvesting honey can be used to make candles and lip balm, too.

home-cooking

honey

candles

Lip balm

Bee aware!

Bees are brilliant **pollinators**, helping new plants to grow. But, just like elephants, bees have lost a lot of their natural habitat. *Find out how you can protect bees on page 46.*

What's inside a beehive?

The type of hive used in a beehive fence is split into two chambers. One side is home to the queen bee, who lays her eggs inside the cells. We call this the **brood**.

The other side is where the **worker bees** store the honey. The worker bees collect **nectar**, bring it back to the hive and turn it into honey, which is kept inside the **honeycomb**.

brood

nectar

honeycomb

The beehive fences keep humans and elephants safe, while making a happy home for the bees and tasty honey for farmers.

3D Space Printing

What do you do when something breaks in space? In order to fix it, you need a special tool but the nearest shop is at least 250 miles away and your home is hurtling through space ...

You 3D print your own, of course!

Not so long ago, astronaut and commander Barry 'Butch' Wilmore was aboard the **International Space Station** (ISS) and needed a new ratchet wrench. He didn't want to wait months, or even years, for a spacecraft to arrive with a resupply of tools. So NASA and a team of engineers on Earth quickly designed a printable wrench.

Butch was able to upload the digital file of printing instructions to the first-ever 3D printer in space, and print his own tool in just a few hours!

What is 3D printing and how does it work?

3D printing is a technology that allows us to print objects.

First, a **digital model** is designed on a computer. This model works like a set of instructions that tell the 3D printer how to print and make an exact copy of the design, using a special type of plastic called **ABS**.

A reel of **plastic filament** is fed into the machine ...

... where it is heated and melted into a mouldable gloop ...

machine

... which is then squeezed out of a nozzle called the **extruder**, building the design one layer at a time from the bottom up.

3D printer

plastic filament

ratchet wrench

extruder

Why do we need to 3D print in space?

Astronauts living and working on board the International Space Station (ISS) need a lot of stuff to be able to sleep, exercise and conduct scientific experiments. The ISS is close enough to Earth to send supplies, but future astronauts will want to voyage further into space.

What then?

A crewed mission to Mars could take years and it's not possible to pack enough supplies to last the entire adventure. This is where 3D printing comes to the rescue. Astronauts will be able to print spare parts for the spaceship, update their tools and might even be able to print clean clothes!

Recycling in space

3D printing stuff in space creates new problems – where will all the old equipment and parts go? There isn't such a thing as a weekly recycling rocket to come and collect the bins.

Astronauts on the ISS are testing a possible solution, a new type of printer called the **Refabricator**. As well as printing new objects, it can also recycle waste plastic and old 3D-printed pieces BACK into plastic filament to create new tools and parts!

Refabricator

Eco-bricks

How do you build a school out of rubbish? High in the remote cloud forests of Guatemala, a group of local farmers, children and volunteers have gathered. Surrounded by luscious wildlife, the community is working hard to build a new school for the village, but they aren't using bricks or wood, or even straw, to construct the walls. They're using plastic bottles stuffed with rubbish!

It's tricky to collect rubbish from mountain villages this high up, so plastic waste builds up and spoils the beautiful environment. But plastic can be a handy material – it's strong and waterproof and lasts a long time. So, this community has decided to put their waste to good use by making eco-bricks!

What is an eco-brick?

An eco-brick is a building block made from a used plastic bottle filled with **non-recyclable waste**. This might include things like **single-use plastic** bags, straws, crisp packets, sweet wrappers and cling film.

First, clean and dry your plastic filling . . .

. . . then use a long stick to poke as much plastic as possible into the bottle.

plastic bottles

Any size of plastic bottle will work, but it's a good idea to use bottles that are often used and easily found in your area. It's much easier to build with lots of eco-bricks that are the same size.

single-use plastic

Eco-bricks are a really simple way for local communities to turn their plastic waste into strong, affordable building materials and prevent it from becoming **pollution**. Instead of a growing rubbish pile, this village has a brand-new school!

Eco-brick engineering

All over the world, eco-bricks are being used to make incredible constructions.

In Guatemala, schools are built by tying eco-bricks to chicken wire. The walls are smothered in cement for extra strength. A roof of corrugated iron is added, and the whole building is supported by a wooden frame.

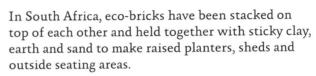

In South Africa, eco-bricks have been stacked on top of each other and held together with sticky clay, earth and sand to make raised planters, sheds and outside seating areas.

In the UK, one school recycled 2 tonnes of plastic by squashing it into 3,000 eco-bricks and built an outside classroom.

Other groups in the UK have used them to construct a wildlife pond, beach huts and even a long wavy bench that looks like a snake!

Eco-bricks are an opportunity to transform plastic waste that could have a negative impact on the planet into something positive.

When we get rid of plastic, some of it might be recycled into new things but sadly lots of it will end up being burned, thrown into **landfill** or swept into the ocean.

Plastic is designed to be strong and long-lasting, but when it's thrown away it breaks down very slowly, releasing harmful chemicals and creating *microplastics* that pollute the environment. However, if we reuse it, we can protect the planet and make loads of cool new stuff.
Check out some ideas on pages 47 and 49!

T-shirt Trends

What if you could make T-shirts from T-shirts?
One billion items of clothing are made each year, but almost 40% never even get worn! This means a dumper truck of perfectly good material gets burned or buried in a huge hole in the ground, called a **landfill**, every second.

£14.99

Clothes can sit in landfills for over 200 years. As they slowly break down, methane is produced. This **greenhouse gas** traps heat in the Earth's atmosphere, causing **global warming**. We can help prevent this by reducing the amount of clothes we buy, reusing clothes from second-hand shops and recycling the ones we already own!
Check out a fun idea on page 47.

Check out a fun idea on page 47.

Landfill

Long live your T-shirt!

Wouldn't it be great if we only made clothes that were really needed, and could find a way to turn old clothes into new ones? One clothing company is trying to solve this very problem and their story starts in India . . .

cotton

renewable energy

Manufacturing

On an **organic** cotton farm in northern India, cotton plants are watered with rainwater and fed with cow manure to help them grow big and strong.

The cotton is picked, cleaned, spun into yarn, woven, cut AND sewn into T-shirts all by the same producers. This means material doesn't get moved around from place to place unnecessarily. The factory is even powered by **renewable energy** sources.

The T-shirts are then shipped to the Isle of Wight, UK, ready for printing.

cow manure

container ship

Ordering

Using **smart technology**, the UK factory only prints a T-shirt when an order has been placed by a customer online.

A factory worker finds the right size and colour T-shirt from the stock room.

Every T-shirt is given a **barcode sticker** that holds all the information about the customer's order. The barcode tells the printer what design to print.

This **digital printer** is powered by renewable energy. It cleverly uses the right amount of ink for the design. None is wasted.

The printed T-shirt is placed on to a hot, flat iron to set and seal the ink.

Once checked, the T-shirt zooms off to the packaging department.

Rather than using plastic bags that could litter our planet for hundreds of years while they break down, the T-shirt is put into an envelope made from **recycled paper** that can be composted or recycled again.

Finally, the T-shirt is sent to its new owner, who can wear it time after time until it's been worn out or outgrown.

But . . . then what happens to it?

Every single T-shirt the factory prints is designed so that it can be sent back in the post to be shredded, recycled and remade into new products again and again.

This is what's known as a **circular economy**.

It works in one big **sustainable** loop!

Seaweed Wraps

What can you make with seaweed? Off the coast of California, USA, beneath the waves, is an underwater garden bathed in aqua-blue light. Skyscrapers of slippery seaweed sway in the flowing current, shellfish cling to the green towers, fish dart between their shadows, and curious otters hunt for sea urchin snacks!

This is a giant **kelp farm** and it produces one of the most **sustainable** foods on the planet – seaweed.

But seaweed isn't only being farmed for food such as sushi wraps. Scientists have found ways to turn it into something else. **Packaging!**

harbour seals

sea otters

What is kelp?

Kelp is a type of brown **algae**, but we mostly call it seaweed. Algae are living organisms that are found all over the world, and although they can look like underwater plants, they are neither plant nor animal.

However, like plants, they do make their own energy using water, sunlight and carbon dioxide. This process is called **photosynthesis**.

spiny lobster

Why is seaweed sustainable?

In a world where waste plastic and **pollution** are growing problems, seaweed is a smart, sustainable solution.

Plastic takes a long time to break down (a few hundred years in some cases), littering our oceans and piling high on **landfill** sites. But seaweed packaging is **biodegradable**. It can be broken down by bacteria, bugs and other living organisms in 4 to 6 weeks.

Not only that, if it is edible, it doesn't need to be thrown in the bin at all. It can be eaten as part of your meal, and your digestive system does the rest!

How is seaweed packaging made?

The kelp is harvested and brought to shore on boats.

It is then washed, dried and ground down into a fine powder.

Next, the powder is blended with water and a few other special ingredients to make a seaweed sludge.

The sludge mixture is heated and boiled, then turned into a thick gloopy gel.

Once the gel has cooled, it can be moulded into something that looks and feels like plastic.

The seaweed 'plastic' can be used to make drink pouches, sauce sachets, carrier bags, food wrap, cups, straws and many other things.

Some scientists are even adding different flavours to the material because some seaweed packaging can be eaten!

carbon dioxide → oxygen ← carbon dioxide

oxygen ← → oxygen

Algae allies!

Growing seaweed also helps the environment. Carbon dioxide is a **greenhouse gas** that's causing average temperatures to rise, leading to **climate change**. Thankfully, the oceans and algae are our allies!

Algae can be microscopic or enormous like seaweed. But no matter the size, it soaks up carbon dioxide to make energy through photosynthesis.

This process helps tackle climate change because it takes carbon dioxide out of our atmosphere, all while growing healthy food and material for us to use and eat.

Seaweed farmers

Finding more uses for seaweed is great news for farmers. Seaweed grows along shorelines worldwide; it doesn't need to be fed or watered and it grows really fast. Giant kelp can grow about 60 cm a day. This means lots can be grown very quickly!

10,000 Mile Shoes

Mount Kilimanjaro

Did you know that tyres can be turned into shoes?
In the foothills of Mount Kilimanjaro, Tanzania, a group of Maasai herders guide their goats towards an area of scrubland for grazing. As they walk for miles across the savannah, they leave nothing but footprints that look like a motorbike has hopped and skipped its way across the dust. Why?
Their sandals have been crafted from old motorbike tyres.

Maasai herders

Tyres are mostly made of natural rubber, **artificial materials**, fabric and wire. They're strong, flexible and last a long time. A car tyre with a bad puncture might not be fixable, but parts of it can still be used to make a strong, sturdy pair of shoes.

How to make tyre sandals

Across East Africa, recycled tyre sandals are known as '10,000 milers', because they're said to last thousands of miles of walking on rough, stony ground.
A skilled cobbler can carve a new pair of 'made to fit' shoes in about 20 minutes.

First, they cut a piece of tyre the length of the foot . . .

. . . then they carve a sandal pattern.

Next, the cobbler cuts some strips of the inner tyre to make the straps . . .

tyre

. . . and fixes them in place.

The cobbler trims the pins and carves the sides to make sure there are no sharp bits.

Now the sandals are ready to be worn for thousands of miles!

hammer

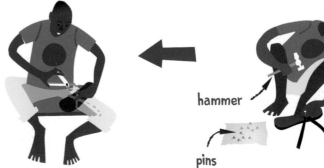

pins

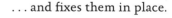

straps

Recycling rubber tyres

Did you know that 1 billion tyres are wasted every year? That's more tyres than people living in the USA! Rubber tyres are large and built to be tough so they take a very long time to break down in **landfill**. They can be burned to make energy, but some of the materials release harmful chemicals and these have to be managed very carefully.

Making sandals is a smart, quick way for local businesses to use rejected tyres. They can be recycled into other things, too. Some big factories are shredding used tyres into lots of tiny pieces called **rubber crumb** that can be used to make playground flooring, sports tracks and even pavements!

rubber tree

The rubber tree

One of the materials used to make tyres is **natural rubber** that comes from a rubber tree.

Natural rubber starts out as a white, gooey liquid called **latex**, that can be found inside the tree's bark.

In a process called **tapping**, a piece of bark is carefully scraped away . . .

bark

. . . and the liquid oozes out, which is collected in a cup.

When the latex meets the air, it turns into a solid, squidgy material that can be sent to factories and made into lots of different things, such as bath toys, party balloons, wellies and tyres!

Latex

A lot of natural rubber goes into making new tyres. With so many old tyres being thrown away every year, recycling them and reusing this precious **natural resource** is very important.

Super Salad

Most plants need soil to grow, right? Well, what if I told you that you can grow the plants for your favourite salad in a tank of water, with just a splash of fish wee to help it along?

In the city of Brighton, UK, a steamy glasshouse is rich with salad leaves, vegetables and fresh fruit that tumble out of baskets, barrels and bamboo pipes. The gentle sound of flowing water can be heard, and when you look closer you'll notice that the plants aren't growing in soil, but instead have their roots dangling in tanks full of fish!

This greenhouse, like others around the world, uses **aquaponics** to grow its plants.

What is aquaponics and how does it work?

Aquaponics is an **ecosystem** where fish, plants and bacteria live and work together. The plants are fed by the fish waste, and the plants and bacteria help clean the water for the fish.

A fish called tilapia

In the wild, fish called tilapia live in rivers, lakes and streams. They like to eat algae and aquatic plants.

They are also a good source of **protein**, which people need as part of a healthy diet. This makes them a popular choice of fish to farm.

tilapia

pump

Aquaponic farmers feed their tilapia fish-food pellets or even leftover leaves and vegetables, so nothing goes to waste.

The fish digest their food and need to wee and poo!

A chemical called **ammonia** is released in their urine (wee) and through their gill Too much ammonia i harmful to the fish, so the water has to be regularly cleaned.

Aquaponics makes it possible to both grow fresh vegetables and farm fish in a **sustainable** way without needing much space. The system works in a cycle so, other than feeding the fish, it doesn't need much looking after. The only thing that goes into the system once it's set up is the fish food! There's no need to add fertilizer to help the plants grow as the fish waste does the job, and the plants and bacteria clean the water so it can be reused again and again.

The plants suck up the water and nitrates through their roots, and the now clean, ammonia-free water drips back into the fish tank for the cycle to start again!

Then another type of bacteria turns the **nitrItes** into **nitrAtes**, which, luckily for us, plants need to stay healthy.

The rough, bumpy surface of the stones makes the perfect home for bacteria. One type of bacteria breaks down the ammonia and turns it into something called **nitrites**.

For thousands of years in southern China and south-east Asia, farmers have been growing rice plants in paddy fields using aquaponics. The farmers flood their fields with water from nearby rivers and marshes, and put fish in the water to eat the bugs and fertilize the plants. When the rice crop is ready for harvesting, the farmers drain the fields and have both rice and fresh fish to eat.

media

roots

The dirty water is pumped up to a grow bed. Plants sit among small stones called **media**, with their roots dangling in the dirty water.

Worm Tea Compost

How many wiggly worms does it take to eat your leftovers?
People have been using **compost** to grow healthy plants, fruits and vegetables for years. And there's a creature that gives us a helping hand, even though it doesn't have any hands itself . . .

. . . **the wiggly worm**!

In the wild, earthworms naturally break down soil, so it's possible to use them in a controlled space, such as a **worm bin**, to break down *organic* waste and make compost. This process is called **vermicomposting**.

Why have a worm bin?

When worms eat your unwanted kitchen waste, they transform it into a nutrient-rich mixture of compost and worm poo that growing plants love.

The best thing is that you can use vermicompost to grow new plants, and when you've eaten those you can feed the leftovers to the worms and the cycle begins again.

The system works in one flowing loop where all the waste is recycled and turned into something useful.

damp mat to keep everything wet

worms

bedding for worms

top tub

holes to allow any liquid to drip out

bottom tub

The bottom tub collects the liquid that drips from above and often has a tap to drain the juices. This liquid comes from all the decomposing materials and is sometimes called **worm tea**! Yuck!

bottom liner to stop worms from falling through the holes

food scraps

Lid with air holes to keep pests out but let the worms breathe

Worms are impressive eating machines! Some composting worms eat almost their body weight in rotting greens each day. That's about the same as an eight-year-old child eating an entire sack of spuds in 24 hours!

How does it work?

There are around 3,000 species of earthworm worldwide, but the types used in vermicomposting are known as **compost worms**. The Red Wiggler is an excellent compost worm because it loves a menu of rotting vegetables and the cosy conditions of a worm bin!

Inside the bin, worms feed on the food scraps and turn them into worm poo. Tiny **micro-organisms** that we can't see, such as fungi and bacteria, also help break down the scraps into smaller pieces. We call it **decomposing**.

History of worms

When the T-Rex roamed the land and pterosaurs soared through the skies more than 66 million years ago, earthworms were there, too, squirming through the soil, recycling leaves, dead wood and dinosaur dung!

Cleopatra (69–30 BCE), the last pharaoh of Ancient Egypt, recognized the importance of earthworms. She took them so seriously she made smuggling earthworms out of Egypt a crime punishable by death!

Charles Darwin (1809–1882) was fascinated by earthworms, too. In one of his books, he wrote, 'It may be doubted whether there are many other animals which have played so important a part in the history of the world.'

worm tea makes great fertilizer for plants!

Composting is great because it reduces the amount of food waste we send to **landfills**. When our leftovers sit in landfills, they create **greenhouse gases** like methane, which contribute to **global warming**. If they can decompose into compost at home, those harmful gases are reduced. It's also a great way to get a free, **sustainable** fertilizer you can feed to growing plants!

Floating Bins

Have you ever noticed rubbish floating in the sea?
If you take a stroll through Sydney Harbour Marina, Australia, and peer over the edge
of a dock, you might see a bright yellow bin bobbing up and down between the boats.
This is a **floating bin** and, just like a litter bin on land, it collects rubbish floating in the water.

The floating bin was the invention of two Australian surfers, Andrew Turton and Pete Ceglinski.
They grew up swimming, sailing and surfing in the ocean, but became so fed up with the
enormous amount of plastic littering their watery playground that they decided to do
something to help. They named their floating bin the **Seabin** and made it their
mission to help clean up the ocean.

How does it work?

A floating bin can move up and down with
the tide. A pump sucks in water and any litter.
Then the water is pumped back into the marina,
leaving the litter trapped in the bag.

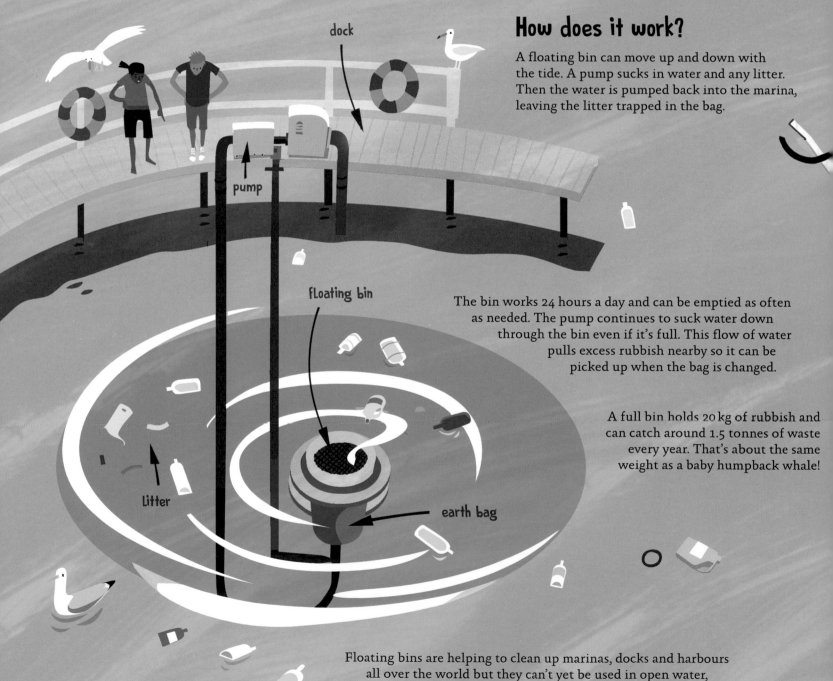

dock

pump

floating bin

Litter

earth bag

The bin works 24 hours a day and can be emptied as often
as needed. The pump continues to suck water down
through the bin even if it's full. This flow of water
pulls excess rubbish nearby so it can be
picked up when the bag is changed.

A full bin holds 20 kg of rubbish and
can catch around 1.5 tonnes of waste
every year. That's about the same
weight as a baby humpback whale!

Floating bins are helping to clean up marinas, docks and harbours
all over the world but they can't yet be used in open water,
and sadly that's where a lot of our plastic waste ends up . . .

Plastic in the ocean

Can you believe that over 8 MILLION tonnes of plastic enter the world's oceans each year? This vast amount of waste causes a big problem for marine life. Animals sometimes get caught up in it or end up mistaking it for food. Most plastics in the ocean break up into tiny bits called **microplastics** that are less than 5 mm long.

the Great Pacific Garbage Patch

microplastics

What happens to plastic in the ocean?

When plastic is washed out to sea, it gets caught up in moving water patterns called **currents**. Currents that swirl in circles are called **gyres**, and they gather pieces of rubbish till they form MASSIVE patches of waste. **The Great Pacific Garbage Patch** is three times the size of France . . .

sea anchor

The Ocean Cleanup

A young Dutch inventor called Boyan Slat and his company have designed an ingenious system – **The Ocean Cleanup**. This U-shaped floating barrier sits on the surface of the water with a 'skirt' that hangs below. The 'skirt' prevents rubbish from escaping. It moves with the wind and the currents, catching plastic waste swirling in the gyres.

They also launched a machine called the **Interceptor**, which uses barriers and a moving conveyor belt to collect floating pieces of rubbish in rivers before they reach the open sea.

plastic

U-shaped barrier

skirt

If you want to help clean up our oceans, just like a floating bin, then why not go on a **litter pick-up** near where you live?

What can we do?

Floating bins and other waste-collection inventions are doing a brilliant job cleaning up marine plastic **pollution**, but it would be wonderful if they were no longer needed in the future. The best thing we can do to achieve this is reduce the amount of **single-use plastic** we use.

MeatLess Burgers

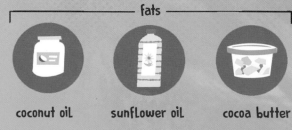

Have you ever eaten a burger that looks and tastes like meat, but was made from plants? Of course, plant-based burgers aren't new – vegetarian burgers have existed for a very long time, but more recently food scientists have figured out how to make plants mimic the look, taste, texture, smell and even the sound of cooking meat!

The great thing about **meatless burgers** is that they can be enjoyed by people who eat a plant-based diet but might also encourage meat lovers to try a veggie option.

Who wants a burger?

First, the burger needs **protein**. Proteins help our bodies repair themselves. Animal products like beef, pork, eggs and fish are high in protein, but so are lots of plants, such as peas, brown rice and soy beans. These plant proteins give the burger a soft, chewy bite that's similar to the experience of eating meat.

   proteins

peas   brown rice   soy beans

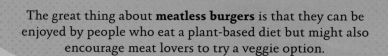

fats

coconut oil   sunflower oil   cocoa butter

Then it needs **fat**. Fats and oils help our bodies store energy, and provide insulation to keep us warm. Plant fats make the burger juicy on the inside and a little crunchy on the outside. And they sizzle on the grill!

Next up are **carbohydrates** to give us energy. These can be found in foods such as bread, potatoes and pasta. In a meatless burger, potato helps to hold the other ingredients together so it can be shaped into a patty.

In animals, **haem** is an important part of the protein **haemoglobin**, which can be found in your blood carrying oxygen around the body. Haem contains lots of iron, which is what gives red meat its slightly metallic taste and pink colour.

Haem can be found in plant proteins, too. Food scientists have discovered a way to take haem from the roots of soy plants and add it to burgers for that all-important pink colour and meaty taste.

But haem isn't the only way to add colour and flavour. Some meatless burgers use a mix of plants like beetroot, red apples and pomegranate.

How do meatless burgers help the planet?

Most meat burgers are made of beef, but eating beef has a big impact on the environment. Let's find out why . . .

Burps and farts – There are around 1.5 billion cows on the planet and all of them need to burp! When a cow digests food, it produces methane, a harmful **greenhouse gas**, that is belched into the atmosphere.

Land – Farming cows takes up a LOT of space. It's said that 26% of all land on Earth is used for grazing livestock. In fact, 80% of the trees cut down in the Amazon rainforest were to make way for cow farms.

Water – The production of beef uses a lot of water. There's drinking water for the cows, the water needed to grow their food, and the water used for cleaning and running the farm.

Not all of us can or will want to cut meat out of our diets completely, but making an effort to reduce the amount we eat will really help the planet!

It takes about 1,500 litres of water to produce 1 kg of wheat and an astonishing 10 times more to produce the same amount of beef!

The problem is that all this is a very inefficient way to produce food. We grow the plants, the animals eat the plants, and then we eat the animals. We could just eat the plants and save lots of the energy that goes into feeding and looking after the animals! That would really reduce greenhouse gases and use up fewer limited resources, too.

41

MagLev Trains

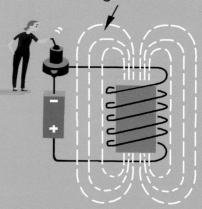

Is it possible for a train to levitate? You'd have to travel to Asia to find out! Imagine arriving in Shanghai, China – you want to get from the airport to downtown Longyang Road and start exploring the city. You could walk the 30 km, but that would take 6 hours. A taxi would take half an hour, or you could catch the train, which will take less than 8 minutes!

Once on board, as if by magic, the train starts to hover and levitates above the track as it hurtles through Shanghai at 431km per hour, making it the quickest passenger train in the world.

It's not magic – it's magnets!

This is a **maglev** train and it works thanks to **magnetic levitation**, a technology that uses magnets and their invisible forces to lift a train off its tracks.

Magnets attract and repel other magnets and some metal objects. Have you ever held two magnets close together and felt them push and pull each other?

The two ends of a magnet are known as the **north pole** and **south pole**, and each end is surrounded by an invisible area called a **magnetic field**.

Transport is a huge source of **noise** and **air pollution**. Maglev trains are extremely eco-friendly, quiet and super speedy. Instead of burning fuel to power an engine, they run using electricity so they don't produce harmful **greenhouse gases**.

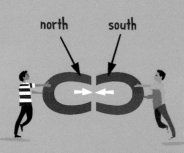

north   south

When the opposite poles of two magnets go into each other's magnetic fields, they pull together. We call this force **attraction**.

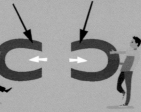

north   north

When two poles of the same kind go into each other's magnetic fields, they are pushed away. We call this **repulsion**.

Electromagnets behave in a similar way, but they are only magnetic when electricity runs through a coil of wire. Switch the electricity on, and it's magnetic. Switch the electricity off, and it's not!

magnetic field

How do maglev trains work?

The track for a maglev train is called a **guideway**, and inside it is an electromagnet. When the electromagnet is powered up, it repels the magnets on the train's undercarriage.

The train's weight pulls it down towards the Earth, but when the magnetic force is strong enough the repulsion lifts the train up to 10cm above the guideway.

Once the train is lifted, electricity is supplied to other electromagnets in the guideway walls. This creates a system of magnetic fields that push and pull the train along the guideway.

Faster than a shooting arrow

Unlike a train with wheels that run on a track, a maglev train hovers on an invisible magnetic cushion. Without the grinding of wheels on metal, or slippery wet leaves to get in the way, a maglev train can travel at super-high speeds!

The Shanghai Maglev travels around 4 times faster than a sprinting cheetah.

But the highest speed of a maglev train was recorded in Japan in 2015, when it reached 603 km per hour. That's nearly twice as fast as a shooting arrow!

The guideways are often raised above the ground, which is less disruptive to the natural environment. As the trains hover above the track rather than screech along it like regular train wheels, they make less noise pollution, too!

Magic Ink

How do you turn pollution into a pen?

Not long ago, at a roadside stall in New Delhi, India, an engineering student called Arpit Dhupar ordered his favourite sugar-cane juice drink. To make it, the seller squeezed the juice from the cane using a machine powered by a diesel generator.

The student noticed that the generator's exhaust pipe had blown soot on to the wall behind it, painting it black.

This mess gave him an idea. What if the soot could be used to paint things on purpose? What if it could be turned into **ink**?

So, Arpit and his friends invented a special type of **filtering machine** that could trap the soot.

The filter attaches to a generator's exhaust pipe and captures the tiny particles of soot in a special liquid before they escape into the air.

The dirty liquid is then collected, cleaned and turned into ink. This ink is used not only in pens but in enormous printers, too.

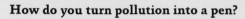

गन्ने का रस
SUGAR-CANE JUICE

soot

diesel generator

Why is soot bad for the environment?

Pollution is when our environment is affected by waste on land, in the sea or up in the air.

Most air pollution comes from burning **fossil fuels** that release **greenhouse gases** such as carbon dioxide into the air. Sometimes this also produces soot.

Soot is sticky and clings to cars, chimneys and walls. It also gets blown into the air and hangs there as **smog**.

In big cities like New Delhi, there can be a lot of smog, which isn't very healthy to breathe.

That's why engineers, scientists and designers in India are dreaming up creative ways to clean the air!

Car inks

One team of engineers in Bangalore, India, has developed a similar filter gadget that attaches to the end of a car's exhaust pipe to collect the soot. When the device is full, the soot can be emptied, cleaned and turned into ink and paint.

When the filter is attached to a running car for 45 minutes, it collects enough soot to make 30ml of ink. That, in turn, could fill about 111 ballpoint pens!

The ink is used for printing on packaging and clothes, and to fill felt-tip pens, which are used by artists around the world.

Soot tiles

A designer from Mumbai, India, has even used soot to make building materials. Local craft workers mix the soot with cement, marble chips and water. They pour the mixture into moulds and bake it in a very hot oven until it hardens to become a beautiful tile.

What could you invent?

The best way to reduce air pollution would be to stop burning fossil fuels in the first place. But while the world moves slowly towards cleaner, **renewable energy**, it's a smart idea to clean up the waste we produce and upcycle it into something we can use! Making ink out of soot is just one way to do it. What pollution-preventing invention might you dream up?

Stuff to Make and Do

Phew! What a journey – we've travelled all around the world, and even into space! On our way, we've discovered **extra**ordinary stories that show us just how inventive humans can be. All this stuff forms part of our everyday lives and, when used in a **sustainable** way, it can really help our planet.

I love finding and reading stories about the way things are made, but sometimes it's fun to make things myself, too! Here are ten super ideas for things you can make using recycled and easy-to-get materials. Each activity has been inspired by one of the stories in this book. Let these ideas be your guide, but why not tweak them and come up with your own designs? Who knows? Maybe you'll invent something amazing!

Find me, 'Maddie Moate', on YouTube and watch all these activities online!

Happy tinkering!

Build a Bumblebee 'n' B
Inspired by Honey Bee Fences

Stuff you need: Clay pot with drainage hole, moss, dry grass and stones.

1. Find a clay plant pot with a drainage hole in the bottom. Put a piece of moss at the bottom of the pot. This will help to keep everything inside dry if it rains.

2. Next, loosely stuff some dried grass into the pot. Add just the right amount so that when you turn the pot over, the piece of moss drops a little to make space for a bumblebee to crawl in.

3. Choose a warm sheltered location, such as the foot of a hedge or a quiet corner of the patio.

4. Turn the pot upside down and fix it in place. You could do this by pushing it down a few centimetres into the soil or surrounding it with moss and stones to hold it down.

5. In the autumn and early winter, queen bumblebees search for warm and dry holes to rest in. Your Bumblebee 'n' B could be the perfect spot! Remember always to observe bees from afar and don't get too close.

Craft your own recycled paper
Inspired by Elephant-Poo Paper

Stuff you need: Old paper, bowl, water, tea towel and rolling pin.

1. Get some recycled paper and tear it into teeny-tiny pieces.

2. In a bowl, mix the pieces of paper with some water. Squish it all together until it's really mushy.

3. Squeeze the mushy mixture into balls of pulp.

4. Place your pulp ball on a flat surface and put a tea towel over the top.

5. Use a rolling pin to flatten the pulp and squeeze out the excess water.

6. Leave the pulp to dry and – ta-da – you have made your own paper!

Construct a compost bin
Inspired by Worm Tea Compost

Stuff you need: Old plastic bottle, scissors, pin, tray, brown/green waste, spray water bottle and kitchen towel.

1. Find an old plastic bottle, give it a wash and peel off any labels.

2. Ask a grown-up to help you cut the top off the bottle and use a pin to poke some holes in the bottom for drainage.

3. Place the bottle on a plastic tray and add a layer of brown waste – like shredded paper, torn-up egg cartons and crunchy old leaves. Spray the brown layer with water till it's damp, but not too soggy!

4. Now add a layer of green waste – like vegetables, food scraps and grass cuttings.

5. Place the tray and composter somewhere warm such as a sunny windowsill. Every day give it a stir and add a little more water to help the **micro-organisms** break the contents down into compost.

6. When you're not mixing the compost, lay a sheet of kitchen towel over the top to keep it nice and damp.

7. Continue to add layers of brown and green waste as days go on, but remember it will take time for everything to decompose, so be patient.

8. When the layers have transformed into compost, you can add it to the soil around your growing plants to give them a healthy snack packed with nutrients!

Tie a T-shirt bag
Inspired by T-shirt Trends

Stuff you need: Old T-shirt and scissors.

1. Find a well-loved T-shirt that won't be worn any more.

2. Ask a grown-up to help you cut off the sleeves and neckline with some scissors. This will form the opening and handles of your bag.

3. Cut 5 cm slits along the bottom of the shirt at the front and back, so it looks like it has a fringe along the bottom.

4. Take the front and back of each strip and tie them together in tight knots.

5. If there are big gaps between the knots, tie some of them together to close them up!

6. Leave the dangly tassels hanging or turn the bag inside out to hide them. Your bag is ready to use!

Sowing seeds without soil
Inspired by Super Salad

Stuff you need: Eggshells, felt-tip pen, cotton wool, cress seeds, a spray water bottle and scissors.

1. With your grown-up, hard boil some eggs and enjoy them for breakfast! Try to crack the shell near the pointy end before you tuck in.

2. Carefully clean the shell and let it dry. (If you don't want to use eggs, you could use toilet-roll tubes instead.)

3. Use a felt-tip pen to draw a funny face if you want the cress to look like hair!

4. Fill the empty shell with damp cotton wool and sprinkle some cress seeds on top.

5. Put your eggshell in a sunny place and spray it with water if it starts to look dry.

6. In just a few days, the cress seeds will sprout and your egg will start to grow hair!

7. When the leaves are a few centimetres long, you can give your cress head a trim with some scissors and sprinkle the leaves on salads and sandwiches. Delicious!

Design your own reusable cup
Inspired by Clay Cups and 10,000 Mile Shoes

Stuff you need: Old glass jar and rubber bands.

1. Ask your grown-up for an empty old glass jar with a wide rim and lid. Then clean it thoroughly.

2. Find some old rubber bands to fit snugly round the jar – the more colours, the better!

3. Layer the rubber bands round the jar in your own colourful design. The rubber bands will act as a natural insulator, keeping your drinks cool.

Bake a veggie burger!
Inspired by Meatless Burgers

Stuff you need: A bowl, a tin of black beans, leftover veggies, flour and tomato paste/ketchup.

1. In a bowl, mix together a tin of black beans, a handful of leftover cooked veggies, 4 tbsp of flour, and 3 good squirts of tomato paste or ketchup!

2. Mash the ingredients into a thick paste.

3. Form little balls out of the paste and flatten them on a baking tray drizzled with a little oil.

4. With your grown-up, bake them in the oven for 20 minutes at 180 °C.

5. When your veggie burgers are ready, eat them as they are or sandwich them in a bun with your favourite toppings. YUM!

Make your own water butt
Inspired by Fog Catchers

Stuff you need: Empty milk/juice container, acrylic paints/waterproof decorations and screws/strong tape.

1. Ask your grown-up for a large milk or juice container (4–6 pints) and its lid. Remove the label and clean it thoroughly.

2. Ask your grown-up to carefully cut off the base.

3. Decorate the bottle with acrylic paints and waterproof decorations. Remember – the water butt will be fixed upside down with the lid at the bottom.

4. Ask your grown-up to securely attach the bottle to a post or fence outside – remember, it could get heavy with water! Leave enough room under the lid to collect your water and make sure the lid is screwed on tight.

5. Wait for rain and watch as your water butt fills up! When you need to water your plants, unscrew the lid and carefully fill up your watering can.

Ginger Lemonade
Inspired by Plant Power

Stuff you need: Ginger, measuring cup, honey, 3 lemons, ice and a jug.

1. Ask your grown-up to peel and slice about 1 inch of ginger.

2. In a heatproof measuring cup, ask your grown-up to mix the ginger with 250 ml of boiling water and 60 ml of honey. Stir well until the honey is dissolved and leave for 10–15 minutes.

3. Squeeze the juice of 3 lemons.

4. Strain the ginger mixture into a jug, add the lemon juice and then fill the jug with water (still or sparkling) and ice. Add more honey or lemon juice to your taste and enjoy your super-healthy ginger drink!

Plastic bag dispenser
Inspired by Eco-bricks

Stuff you need: Empty 2-litre plastic bottle, scissors, paint/decorations and screws or double-sided tape.

1. Reuse an empty 2-litre plastic bottle. Ask your grown-up to cut off the neck and the bottom of the bottle. Give it a good clean!

2. Make two small holes on one side of the bottle, at the top and bottom. This is to hang it up later.

3. Cover your bottle in decorations using paint or stick-on scraps of recycled paper.

4. Ask your grown-up to attach it to the wall and then fill it with your plastic or reusable bags. Pull one through from the bottom and you'll always have a bag ready to go!

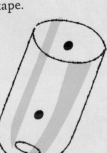

Stuff You Might Need to Know

We all need energy. Energy is a power that makes other things happen. There are lots of different forms of energy including electricity, light, heat, movement and sound. We use energy to heat our homes, keep us cool, cook our food, and loads more stuff.

Types of energy

There are two types of energy we use to power our stuff:

Renewable energy is a source of energy that gets naturally replaced and won't be used up in our lifetime. Wind, water and sunlight are sources of renewable energy that can be used to create electricity.

Non-renewable energy comes from things that can't be replaced. Most of our non-renewable energy sources are fossil fuels.

Fossil fuels: Coal, oil and natural gas are all types of fossil fuels that we burn to power lots of things, from lawnmowers to huge factories. We call them fossil fuels because, like fossils, they are the remains of plants and other living things like prehistoric plankton and dinosaurs that lived hundreds of millions of years ago! This might sound cool, but burning fossil fuels releases greenhouse gases that are harmful to the environment.

Greenhouse gases, such as carbon dioxide and methane, are gases that trap heat in the Earth's atmosphere. They work a little bit like a greenhouse: they let sunlight in but make it tricky for heat to escape. Our planet needs some greenhouse gases to trap heat, otherwise the Earth would become freezing cold and humans would struggle to survive. But in the past few hundred years humans have been burning LOTS of fossil fuels, which has released LOTS of greenhouse gases into the atmosphere. This has led to our planet warming up faster than ever before.

Global warming happens when temperatures rise around the world. The idea of warmer winters and even hotter summers might sound lovely, but, sadly, when temperatures rise quickly and are uncontrolled, it can have a big impact on our planet's climate. One of the reasons for global warming is the burning of fossil fuels.

Climate change is a change in the planet's weather and temperatures over a long period of time. The Earth's climate has changed a lot in the 4.5 BILLION years it has existed. There have been times when the planet was very hot, and times when it was very cold (that we call the ice ages). These changes to the climate were caused by natural things like volcanic eruptions and they happened over VERY long periods of time. However, in the past few hundred years, climate change has been caused by human activity, such as burning fossil fuels, which has led to global warming at a very fast rate.

So, what are some of the impacts?

→ Warming temperatures are causing glaciers and ice sheets to melt, which leads to rising water levels and flooding.

→ The oceans absorb carbon dioxide, which makes them more acidic. This can be harmful to plants and animals that live in the oceans.

→ Extreme weather events such as heatwaves, droughts and typhoons happen more often and are more intense.

How can we make things better?

Climate change can be an upsetting thing to read about because the impact it has on the natural world makes life tough for humans and wildlife on Earth. But if we can understand climate change we can talk about it and help to make things better!

The **GOOD NEWS** is that by using fewer fossil fuels and releasing less greenhouse gases, we can help to control climate change and reduce the impact it has on our planet.

How do we do this?

This book is full of **extra**ordinary stories about ordinary things that are **sustainable**. When something is sustainable, it has usually been made in a way to make sure that it lasts a very long time, or has been made with resources that will bring as little harm to the environment as possible.

When living sustainably, we are making sure that resources will still be available for other people in the future. All the stuff you have read about in this book is sustainable, such as packaging made from seaweed or incredible inventions that harness the weather.

Three Rs for Planet Earth

Reduce – We can **reduce** our waste by throwing away less stuff and only buying the things we really need.

Reuse – We can **reuse** our stuff when we use it again and again, or take an old item and find a new use for it.

Recycle – We can **recycle** our stuff when we turn our waste items into new reusable materials. I like to find things in the recycling bin at home and reuse them by turning them into new things before they eventually get recycled!

REDUCE
REUSE
RECYCLE

Glossary

Here are a few more **special words** with a quick description to help you understand the meanings behind them. I really enjoy discovering new words and learning new things, don't you?

Stay curious!

Artificial materials
Artificial materials are created by humans using science and technology and cannot be found naturally.

Biodegradable
Something is biodegradable when it can be broken down or decomposed by tiny living things we call micro-organisms.

Circular economy
A circular economy produces goods while limiting the waste of natural resources, aiming to use renewable sources of energy where possible. It's opposite to a linear economy, which has a 'take, make and dump' model of production.

Conservationists
A conservationist works to protect biological life, natural habitats and ecosystems. There are lots of different types of conservationists but all have the same job – to look after the health of our planet for future generations.

Deforestation
This is the permanent removal of trees to clear land for farming or grazing cattle, or using timber for fuel, construction or manufacturing products. Reforestation is the process of planting trees in a forest where trees have been cut down.

Geothermal energy
Geothermal energy is created from the heat beneath the Earth's crust. It can be harnessed naturally, but it can also be accessed by digging deep wells into the Earth. The heat found there can be used to drive turbines connected to electricity generators. While it is a renewable source, geothermal energy has to be carefully accessed and managed.

Landfill
A landfill is a place to dump waste materials. Not only are they ugly to look at, but they produce harmful greenhouse gases which contribute to global warming. They also pollute the local environment through harmful toxins that leak into the water and soil. Almost two thirds of landfill waste is biodegradable, so the more we can compost and reduce our food waste, the better!

Micro-organisms
Tiny living things, such as bacteria and fungi, that we can't see without a microscope. Micro-organisms help decompose natural materials.

Microplastics
Microplastics are fragments of plastic less than 5 mm – about the same size as a sesame seed. They are broken down from larger bits of plastic, or can come from cosmetics, clothing or industrial processes. These tiny particles are polluting the ocean, freshwater and land, with humans and animals consuming them daily.

Natural resources
Natural resources come from plants, animals or the environment. They are usually either renewable (wind, water, solar energy) or non-renewable (oil, natural gas, coal). We use natural resources to make stuff (paper, glass, plastics), some of which can be recycled and used again. Other natural resources are limited in quantity, like fresh water. It's important to preserve our natural resources as much as we can.

Non-recyclable waste
Non-recyclable waste doesn't break down easily, which causes the build-up of landfills and harmful toxins. When you buy stuff, check to see if the packaging can be recycled. Common non-recyclable waste includes cling film, crisp packets, sweet wrappers, bubble wrap, polystyrene and single-use plastics.

Organic
When we talk about something being organic, we often mean it has been produced without the use of chemical fertilizers, pesticides or other artificial chemicals. It's often associated with food and farming methods and is generally better for the environment.

Pollution
Pollution happens when harmful materials get into the air, water or land. Pollution is toxic to the environment and harmful to all living things. Noise and light pollution also impact human and animal life. This is often caused by machines and transport, which can disrupt the natural environment.

Single-use plastic
Single-use plastic is a common type of non-recyclable waste. It is only used once before it is thrown away. It includes plastic cutlery, straws, cups and most food packaging. Remember the Three Rs and see what you can reduce, reuse or recycle!

Stuff to Spot!

Finding things can be really exciting, especially when you notice something new –
like a tiny mini-beast under a leaf or a star in the sky. Sometimes you
might even find something no one else has ever seen before!

See if you can spot these things in the book. What else can you find?

Keep exploring!

Thor Mouse Cinnamon Shampoo Honey

Row boat Van Ladybird Eagles Monkey

Wheelbarrow Spanner Beetroot Goats Cheetah

Harbour seals Scooter Bacteria

And see if you can spot me on every page, too!

Answers (left to right): page 13, 21, 16, 15, 23, 39, 29, 36, 18, 27, 10, 25, 41, 32, 43, 30, 45, 35.

53